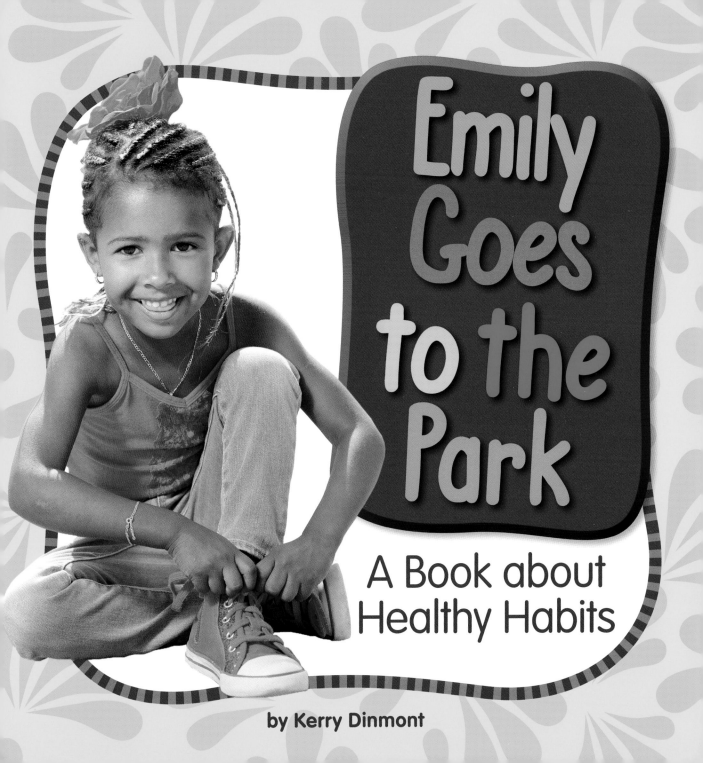

Emily Goes to the Park

A Book about Healthy Habits

by Kerry Dinmont

Published by The Child's World®
1980 Lookout Drive • Mankato, MN 56003-1705
800-599-READ • www.childsworld.com

Photographs ©: Alena Ozerova/Shutterstock Images, cover, 1, 3, 6, 13;
Shutterstock Images, 4–5, 10–11; Carl Stewart/Shutterstock Images, 9;
Balance Photo/Shutterstock Images, 15; Samuel Borges Photography/
Shutterstock Images, 16–17; Svetlana Serebryakova/Shutterstock Images, 19;
iStockphoto, 21

ISBN 9781503820210
LCCN 2016960946

Printed in the United States of America
PA02340

Today, Emily goes to the park.

What healthy choices does she make at the park?

Emily does not go to the park alone. She is safer with an adult and her brother.

She puts on sunscreen. It protects her skin from the sun.

9

She plays soccer with her friends. Running keeps her healthy and strong.

Emily ties her shoes tight. She will not trip.

Emily takes a break. She drinks water. Her body needs water to stay healthy.

Emily is hungry. She washes her hands before she eats. This washes away **germs**.

She eats a banana.
This gives her body
energy.

What do you do to stay healthy?

Glossary

energy (EN-ur-jee) Energy is the ability or strength to do something. A banana is a healthy food that gives your body energy.

germs (JURMZ) Germs are tiny living organisms that can cause disease. We wash our hands before eating to get rid of germs.

Extended Learning Activities

1. It is not safe to go to the park alone. Who do you go to the park with?

2. What healthy habits do you practice each day?

3. Emily plays soccer at the park. What physical activities do you like to do?

To Learn More

Books

Meiners, Cheri J. *Grow Strong! A Book about Healthy Habits*. Minneapolis, MN: Free Spirit Publishing, 2016.

Sjonger, Rebecca. *Do Your Bit to Be Physically Fit!* New York, NY: Crabtree Publishing Company, 2016.

Web Sites

Visit our Web site for links about healthy habits:
childsworld.com/links

Note to Parents, Teachers, and Librarians: We routinely verify our Web links to make sure they are safe and active sites. So encourage your readers to check them out!

About the Author

Kerry Dinmont is a children's book author who enjoys art and nature. She lives in Montana with her two Norwegian elkhounds.